A Beautiful Mind

Poems by

Pamela Martin

A Beautiful Mind
Copyright 2009 by Pamela Gowan

All rights reserved under International and Pan-American copyright conventions. No part of this book may be reproduced, stored in a retrieval system or transmitted in any form, electronic, mechanical, or by any other means, without written permission of the author.

International Standard Book Number: 978-0-578-02010-5

Illustrated by Kathleen Hardy.

Table of Contents

Part I

Borealis	9
"Vixere fortes ante Agamemnona"	9
The Martin Chronicles	9
The Insubordinate Cat	10
In a Quandary	10
"Curiosity may have *thrilled* the cat…"	10
It's good in the "Hood."	11
A Logical Mutation	12
"Trying Times"	12
Sibling Rivalry	12
"A Comedy of Errors"	13
In the Crapper!	14
"No Sign of Forced Entry"	14
Incidental Music	14
The *"Benihana"* of Life	15
"Poetry is Verse"	16
The Master and His Mistress	16
"Fools Rush in…"	16
"Sixty Minutes"	17
A Singed Cat	18
"No Child Left Behind"	18
A Starvation Diet	18
Purseverance	19
Excommunicated	20
Iconography	20
Epigraphy: The Fine Print	20
"The Thing with Feathers"	21
"Bilgistic Love"	21
"Great Expectations"	21
Choate	22
Alone and Confused	22
Harley David's Son	22
"The Memory of Life Lives On"	23
Unintended Consequences	23
A Parent's Lamentation	23
The Conservative Agenda	24
Mind Your Own Business	24

Part II

No Reparations!	27
"The Gift Outright"	27
"Going Green"	27
Voracity	28
Isolationism	28
The Cult of Youthfulness	28
Feminism 101	29
A Song without Words	30
The Addictive Personality	30
Addition and Subtraction	30
The Beatification Process	31
"The Coffee Cantata"	32
A Measured Cadence	32
Madonna and Child	32
A Beautiful Mind	33
The Trepidation	34
Moral Turpitude	34
In the Eleventh Hour	34
Lagging Behind	35
The Deadline	36
"Guernica"	36
Corporate History	36
A Probative Proboscis	37
Nat, King Coal	38
Bon Voyage!	38
A Civil Right	38
Precepts	39
Via Doloroso	39
Elusive	39
"The Apple of Discord"	40
School Daze	40
A posteriori	40
Chaos	41
Matriculation Blues	41
White Supremacy	41
"Sleepless in Chicago"	42

Part III

A Pontification	45
Statutory Rape	45
A Pathology of Lies	45
The Superlative Sex	46
The Sentinel	46
The Past as Prologue	46
The Mother of All Hens	47
The Blessed Redeemer	48
The Virgin	48
An Epiphany	48
Banalities	49
Stream of Consciousness: The Malingerer	50
Under- and Umber-age	51
Dr. Seuss	52
White Lies	52
The "Fair" Fairy	52
A Scripted Life	53
Visionaries	54
A Crass Materialist	54
Perhaps	54
Approaching Montparnasse	55
Trifles	56
"Honest Tea"	56
Serotonin	56
Mauve is My Favorite Color	57
The "Torcher"	57
"Divine Comedies"	57
A Sign of the Times	58
District 101	58
Prologue to *My Autobiography*	58
In the Corner Stoned	59
A Sigh of the Times	59
No Pain, No Gain: "The Opium of the Masses"	59
The Altercation	60
"The Flash"	60

Part I

Borealis*

When that cold north wind
Rears his ugly head,
Then you know for certain
You wish you were dead.
When all is said and done,
I think it's a pity
"Urbs in Horto"+
Is the Windy City.

*Latin, "the north wind;" often the personification of the north wind.
+Latin, "city in a garden," motto of Chicago highlighting Chicago's plethora of "natural life."

*"Vixere fortes ante Agamemnona."**

All is forbidden.
All is verboten.
All is forgiven.
All is forgotten
Except for mighty
Agamemnon
Whose memory lingers
On and on.

*Latin, "There were brave men before Agamemnon." Famous dictum quoted from the *Odes* of the Roman poet Horace (65-8 B.C.). In Greek mythology, Agamemnon led the Greeks to victory during the Trojan War.

The Martin Chronicles

Although you do not know me
Or know me very well,
There's something I must tell you
Before I go to hell.
The only thing that matters
Is hagiography
Or history in the making
For posterity.

The Insubordinate Cat

Tabby has such good
Hand-eye coordination.
It helps make up for her
Insubordination.
When I tell her to sit,
She jumps up instead
And never lets me sleep
In my cozy bed.

In a Quandary

I am at a crossroads.
What choice should I make?
Hang my head in sorrow
Or come to celebrate
What life has to offer.
(It has been so good)
And do all those things
That I know I should?

"Curiosity may have *thrilled* the cat…"

I treat them like cargo
Or a living freight
And take them to the places
They can't overtake.
They can only see
Life from lower grounds
But I say of them,
"Curiosity astounds!"

It's good in the "Hood."

    I have too many books
    And too little cash.
    And I know for certain
    It's all balderdash.
    But if somebody likes it,
    (It's pretty good)
    I will have redeemed
    This fair neighborhood.

A Logical Mutation

If you would only listen
To what I have to say,
We would need no counseling
For which we have to pay.
In one tender moment
We could do away
With this verbal baggage
In a single day.

"Trying Times"

While we pay our taxes,
Death patiently awaits
That one fateful moment
When a life he takes.
Although we may not want to,
We all say goodbye.
It's the only thing
We don't have to try.

Sibling Rivalry

You would think my life
Is a family act.
My *dramatis personae*
Is a given fact.
We are all related.
(Some more than others)
So why do we not act
More like loving brothers?

"A Comedy of Errors"

It's a forgone conclusion.
It's inevitable.
Your destination
Is risible.
Although you don't want it,
That's what you got.
Take it or leave it.
Like it or not.

In the Crapper!

We only fear those things
That we do not know.
I fear everything.
It only goes to show.
But when I'm not afraid,
It makes me so happy
To know that I fear nothing
When I'm feeling crappy.

"No Sign of Forced Entry"

I heard a knocking at the door
And, thinking it was you,
I foolishly unlatched it
But at once I knew
It was a wishful thinking
That had brought me to
This vulnerable position
I could only rue.

Incidental Music

Bollywood is Hollywood
In another place.
On the Indian continent
It is a saving grace.
With or without warning,
They burst into song.
But we do not mind.
We sing right along.

The *"Benihana"* Of Life

I know it's over
But it'd mean a lot
If you'd break it gently
To those who do not.
Timing and delivery
Are everything in life.
I know too well
They can cut like a knife.

"Poetry is Verse"*

My poetry consists
Of insobriety
That makes my life more bearable
In society.
I know there's a reason
He blessed with me with verse.
But there are times
I think it's a curse.

*Part of the adage: "A pun is the lowest form of humor but poetry is verse."

The Master and His Mistress

Pardon me for saying
What I write is trash.
But it's written in the genre
Of my hero Ogden Nash.
His was so much better.
The New Yorker published it.
And I don't have to tell you
I liked it quite a bit.

"Fools Rush in…"

I knew when I met you
You would drive me mad.
But you're the only lover
I have ever had.
Practice makes perfect.
Perfection is best
When subjected to reality
And put to the test.

"Sixty Minutes"

"Sanctus, Sanctus, Sanctus,"*
Did the angels sing
Of the Holy Trinity.
What hope they did bring.
In our time of sorrow
They will intercede
And be there tomorrow
In our hour of need.

*Latin, from Revelation 4:8: "Holy, Holy, Holy" from the Vulgar Bible.

A Singed Cat

I took a trip to the sun.
Boy, did I get burned.
But, as I approached it,
This is what I learned:
Objects look much closer
Than they really are
Especially when it comes
To a dying star.

"No Child Left Behind"

I want to be that person
That I always was.
I want to be just like her
If only because
The times, it seems, are changing.
Please, turn back the clock.
But that ship has sailed
And left me at the dock.

A Starvation Diet

Pretty and smart, they love fine art.
What more can I say?
I give them the best. They won't settle for less
Much to my dismay.
They won't eat their food. I think it's rude
To act this way.
They can hunger strike for as long as they like
As they waste away.

Purseverance*

If I predecease you
(That means I die first),
Will you spend my money
On a wretched hearse?
I'm not a man of wisdom
But I am averse
To loosening the strings
Of my modest purse.

*A neologism combining the nouns "purse" and "severance."

Excommunicated

I took you for granted.
And I must admit
I left without warning
In a raging fit.
Although you have banned me
From your present life,
Would you, please, acknowledge
I was once your wife?

Iconography

I like the "save" icon.
I like it a lot.
And there are times
I think it is hot
Like when I have failed to
Or when I cannot
Remember that something
I have forgot.

Epigraphy: The Fine Print

I'll know it when I see it.
But for now I'm blind
To the simple truths
I have left behind.
Nothing lasts forever
Least of all true love.
It's written in the heavens
And the stars above.

"The Thing with Feathers"*

"The business of business is business."
By that I mean to say
You are my only business.
Don't send me away.
If you do not want me,
That is for today.
I'll be back tomorrow.
It's a brand new day.

*From the first line of a poem by Emily Dickinson entitled, "Hope."

"Bilgistic Love"*

You want me to believe
There was once a king
Who ruled throughout England
But gave up everything
To be with his true love,
Who they called a "whore,"
A twice-divorced woman,
Who hailed from Baltimore?

*"Neologism for "crazy love." The true story of Edward VIII (1894-1972), king of England, who abdicated his reason and his throne to marry Wally (i.e. Wallis) Simpson and lived happily ever after—in France!

"Great Expectations"

We all have expectations
That go unfulfilled.
We do our best to meet them
With something we distilled.
There's no prohibition
Hanging o'er our heads
Like the "Sword of Damocles"*
Filling us with dread.

*A looming threat; an uneasiness caused by an impending danger.

Choate

I was once an orphan.
Now I'm all grown up.
It really doesn't matter
Unless I'm out of luck.
Change is universal.
It is confraternal.
Change is life abundant.
It is life eternal.

Alone and Confused

I don't think about the good times
We often had
Because I know it
Would make me sad
To know they were gone
As soon as they began.
As hard as I try,
I don't understand.

Harley David's Son

There are many things
I do not like
Like the roar of thunder
When I fly a kite.
But I can attest
My greatest dislike
Is the thought of you riding
A motorbike.

"The Memory of Life Lives On"

There are no eternal truths.
Eternity is dead,
As dead as a letter
That will go unread.
But if you tell your story
Distinctly, crisp, and clear,
There's no need worry.
You have naught to fear.

Unintended Consequences

Inadvertence is a thing
You do not intend
To tell someone in confidence
Because you can't defend
It in a court of law.
I tell you "mum's the word"
When it comes to hearing
What you should not have heard.

A Parent's Lamentation

If it goes without saying,
(And I can attest)
You have raised your child
And given him your best.
If that's insufficient,
The angels often sing
Of the disappointment
Children often bring.

The Conservative Agenda

Life may have its ups and downs
But the status quo
Is something you should not abide
Because you never know
One day can make the difference
In the scheme of things.
And you can be quite certain
To yesterday it clings.

Mind Your Own Business

People will always tell you
What you do do wrong.
It is my philosophy
Just to get along
Because it stands to reason
They are really blind.
"People who mind don't matter.
People who matter don't mind."*

*The wise words of Theodor Geisel, (1904-91), a.k.a. Dr. Seuss.

Part II

No Reparations!

To bulwark is to buttress
And shore up your defense.
It doesn't take a genius
To make a false pretense.
But I say to you
(I mean no offense)
I have no intention
Of giving recompense.

"The Gift Outright"

You will never know
What you have given me.
You've given me the truth
And set my spirit free.
Truth is not something
To be taken lightly.
Now I am a beacon
Of what love should be.

"Going Green"

Would somebody tell me
What I'm doing here?
I only had one drink
Of Bailey's Irish cheer.
The Irish have a way
Of making just one toast
Last throughout the evening
Or so they boast.

Voracity

Your insatiability
I cannot abide.
You should give it up
Or finally decide
To find another lover
To fulfill your needs.
I have run out
Of worry beads.

Isolationism

Learn to accept
And come to cope
With the idiosyncrasies
Of a confirmed misanthrope.
I have no quarrel
Or enmity
For the kind fellow
Who lets me be.

The Cult of Youthfulness

Hannah is a palindrome
Who can sing and dance
And can calm most restless hearts
With harmless romance.
But I know for certain
This, too, shall pass
For a woman can't well
Compete with a lass.

Feminism 101

He's calling me now
To bring him some food.
What I need now
Is a brief interlude.
Virginia was right.
I need a room of my own
To think in and write in
And be alone.

*1929 feminist treatise by English novelist, Virginia Woolf, which argued that women need two things: a fixed income and "a room of one's own." Woolf's life was made into a motion picture called *The Hours* starring Nicole Kidman (of all people). She committed suicide by weighing herself down with a rock and then flinging herself into the Ouse River near her Sussex home. Symbolic?

A Song without Words

Words cannot express
What went so wrong
As we sang the words
To our favorite song.
Now I sing in silence.
It's accurate to say
You are the reason
I feel this way.

The Addictive Personality

People prefer uppers to downers
Or so it seems.
I came to know this
In my daydreams.
Happiness may seem
Chemically induced
But people really are
Easily seduced.

Addition and Subtraction

I can't deny
It made me mad
To see you with her.
It made me sad.
What if you saw
Me with a cad?
You were the best thing
I ever had.

The Beatification Process

I'm an eclectic.
I'm tolerant to a fault.
But I've been the victim
Of many an assault.
I know my place
Is no place at all.
I belong to the ages
And the cathedral

"The Coffee Cantata"

I made a pot of coffee
For my tired dad.
Without his coffee,
He is a so sad.
This is an example
Of how I have to pander.
But to do otherwise
Would require more than candor.

A Measured Cadence

Sometimes I wonder
If my feet touch the ground.
Why do I march
To that rhythmic sound?
The beat of the drummer
Steadies my soul.
To reach the stars
Makes my drum roll.

Madonna and Child

Daughters are bad.
Sons are worse.
Children are
A family curse.
But for them
There'd be no futures.
But for them
There'd be no moochers.

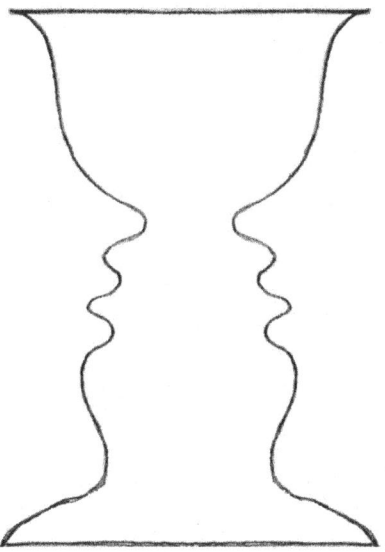

A Beautiful Mind

What you see and what I see
Are two different things.
You look for life's meaning
On angel's wings.
But look a little lower
And surely you'll find
My mind's in the gutter.
I'm so unrefined.

The Trepidation

"Bad hair beats no hair,"
Said the balding man,
"I know it is true.
I do what I can
To keep my hairline
On my forehead.
Hair loss is too real.
It fills me with dread."

Moral Turpitude

Don't impugn my motives
If they aren't as pure
As the driven snow.
You can't be too sure
My moral deficiency
Is decadence.
Depravity is the way
Of all indigents.

In the Eleventh Hour

I prayed to God in the promenade
For eternal redemption.
He told me there would be
No special exception
To the rule that no fool
Will ever go to heaven.
But if I do I say to you
I'll be back by eleven.

Lagging Behind

When you get jet lag
You cannot tell
If you're in London
Or if you're in hell,
If it is day
Or if it is night.
And you never drop off
Without a fight.

The Deadline

It's always hanging
Over your head.
It's not for nothing
They call it "dead."
Infinitely wise,
It annihilates
Any man or woman
Who hesitates.

"Guernica"

It's not a battle.
It is a war
Waging inside
Of our innermost core.
To know there exists
A great iniquity
And to do nothing
Is hypocrisy.

Corporate History

When history lends itself
To the global banker,
She compromises everything
And causes such a rancor.
Through her timely service,
(In the name of greed)
She perpetuates the myth
Until we intercede.

A Probative Proboscis

Frosty was a snowman,
Who lived in the North pole.
Santa gave to him
One precious piece of coal.
A clever boy he was
Making it a nose.
He stuck it on his face
Like Pinocchio's.

Nat, King Coal*

School was something I endured.
It was reprehensible.
But, when I finally became inured,
It was comprehensible.
The moral of this story
Is to stay in school
Until you have become
A reusable fossil fuel.

*a.k.a. Nat King Cole (1917-1965), a popular crooner and jazz pianist, who sang such lyrics as "Mona Lisa, Mona Lisa, men have named you/ You're so like the lady with the mystic smile…" (*Mona Lisa,* 1950*)* and who could forget: "Unforgettable, that's what you are/Unforgettable though near or far.… (*Unforgettable,* 1951, and in a posthumous release recorded and re-mastered with his daughter, Natalie, in 1991).

Bon Voyage!

I have traveled near and far
To distant foreign lands.
But it was not a waste of time
To one who understands
Expanding your horizons
(And I mean literally)
Is the best thing you can do
To fulfill your destiny.

A Civil Right

You're no good for me.
And I'm no good for you.
What do you think
We ought to do?
Give up the ghost
Of civility
And put on the yoke
Of servility?

Precepts

It doesn't take an Einstein
Or a baby Stuey*
To know you use chopsticks
When you eat chop suey.
But you must learn
This elementary principle:
You must obey
Your high school principal.

*An allusion to Stuart Griffin, the precocious infant featured on the long-running animated "sitcom," *The Family Guy,* created by Seth MacFarlane.

*Via Doloroso**

I'm sorry for you.
You're sorry for me.
We both keep
Such sad company.
But someday
Our ship will come in
And our life together
Will finally begin.

*Latin, "the way of sorrow;" the original 'via dolorosa' was the way to Christ's Crucifixion but has now come to mean "a painful or sorrowful experience."

Elusive

I always liked
Clever evasions.
I thought of them as
Quadratic equations.
I write them now
With great ease.
But I think of them
As my disease.

"The Apple of Discord"

What can be more boring
Than eating coconut
For breakfast, lunch, and dinner
In the same old rut?
That's as orthodox
As my lapsed religion.
Everything, it seems,
Is subject to revision.

School Daze

One is one too many.
Two is two too much.
Three is a crowd
Playing double-dutch.
Four is for the foreman.
Five is a fifth of gin.
Six is two plus three.
When does school begin?

*A posteriori**

When somebody tells you
Exactly where to go
And kindly helps you pack
Your leather portmanteau,
Don't bite him in the ass.
That would be ungrateful.
Turn the other cheek,
And be not hateful.

*Logical reasoning from effect to cause based on observation or experience.

Chaos

Listen to
Your inner child
And do something
Considered wild.
I advocate
A gay abandon
Because I think
Life is random.

Matriculation Blues

I'm a free spirit
As free as can be
Sponging off my parents
Constantly.
Finding a job
Is hard to do.
That's why I'm going
Back to school.

White Supremacy

Always wear white
On your wedding day
Because you'll be
On display.
Never wear white
After Labor Day
Because in the snow
You'll fade away.

"Sleepless in Chicago"

Cats are nocturnal.
They play all night.
Then in the morning,
They're out like a light.
Disabuse them of this habit
And surely you'll find
Yourself in the middle
Of something maligned.

Part III

A Pontification

Take it from a professional.
Take it from a pro.
This is the only life
You will ever know.
John said it wisely.
I say after him:
"You have nothing to lose
But your mortal sin."

Statutory Rape

You were my first.
I count the days.
But we have gone
Our separate ways.
Tell me true
Before it's too late.
Was I just
Jail bait?

A Pathology of Lies

You promised in my lifetime
I would not fear
The day would come
When you wouldn't be here.
Now I pine in sorrow
And rue the day
You cruelly told me
You'd go away.

The Superlative Sex

Women are better drivers
If I do say so.
I'm a woman driver.
It's something I should know.
If you don't believe me,
Just give me a test
And put all your doubts
Safely to rest.

The Sentinel

Every day I face the world
Like everybody else.
But there are many things
I hide upon the shelf.
I'm not in the closet.
It's more like a pantry
Filled with disappointments
Guarded by a sentry.

The Past as Prologue

With deliberate haste,
Time fades away.
And when it's gone,
It's gone to stay.
Finding the past
Is hard to do.
But you would try
If it happened to you.

The Mother of All Hens

If I love the one,
I must love the other.
This is the rule
If it's a sister or a brother.
It's form of nepotism
That can't be overstated.
The love of a mother
Cannot be estimated.

The Blessed Redeemer

It's only logical.
The best man should win
A place in our hearts
Because He expiates our sin.

The Virgin

The expert witness
Makes a good defense:
"Let him off easy.
It was his first offense."

An Epiphany

Love is something
I don't understand.
Should it be between
A woman and a man?
Some say, "Yes,"
But I say "Know
Thyself," and
It will show.

Banalities

When we play tug-of-war,
I will always win
Because you are a puny wuss
And I am a gremlin.
I'm the one
Who has the strength
To go the distance
By a length.

Stream of Consciousness: The Malingerer

To gripe is to beach.
To beach is to stay
In the sun too long
On a summer's day.
The days are long,
But the knights are bolder.
You better hurry
Because you're getting older.
I love you.
And you love me.
We get along
So famously.
Tell me now
What would you say
If I tried
To go away?
Would you be sad
And start to cry
Because I gave
No reason why?
Be a sport
And tell me true.
Did I mean
A thing to you?
If two is two
And ten is ten,
When is when
And then is then.
Peter, the griffin,
Is my hero.
Everyone else
Is a zero.
I could go on
But I won't.
It is better
That I don't.

Under- and Umber-age

I slept on a bed of lumber.
Now I have to say I wonder.
When I hear the roar of thunder,
I readjust my "sleep" number.
I made an egregious blunder
When I went too deep in slumber.
But, if that's all I do encumber,
It will put my fears asunder.

Dr. Seuss

They say I know
Thing One and Two
More than I
Should say or do.
If I did not,
I tell them this:
If I did not,
I'd be remiss.

White Lies

Suffering is the only thing
That can bring me down.
Otherwise "yours truly"
Is the perfect clown.
From the clothes on my back
To the shoes on my feet,
Who cares if it involves
A modicum of deceit?

The "Fair" Fairy

There's nothing fair about the Fair
In this state of Grace.
And it may be the best thing
To have happened to this place
If it puts you in a mode
Of quiet excitation
And causes not in anyone
The slightest enervation.

A Scripted Life

I have spoken these same words
At least a dozen times
Enough to know for certain
They do not define
Me as a person
Although I know they could.
But I do not let them
Although I know I should.

Visionaries

My two cats
Have four eyes.
This should come
As no surprise.
Although they use them
With great stealth,
They both know
Their health is wealth.

A Crass Materialist

It is said
I write for cash
Like my hero
Ogden Nash.
But I'm still waiting
For the check.
As yet I have
Not one kopeck!
I need money
More than you.
That is just my
Point of view.
If they tell you
Poetry pays,
Tell them that
I need a raise.

Perhaps

Evil forces lurk about
In every nook and cranny.
Within the darkness of my soul
I think it's uncanny.
We lead lives of turpitude
And unabashed indifference.
Can a man of probity
Really make a difference?

Approaching Montparnasse*

This may be a silly book.
But, if you take a closer look,
You will see that I betook
Not to be a low-life crook.

*The region of Paris where many poets lived; derived from Mount Parnassus, mythological home of the muses.

Trifles

A Trinity
A trilogy.
Three's a crowd.
Three's company.
All good things
Come in three.
Let's all practice
Trigamy.

"Honest Tea"

I read leaves.
I can see.
You are like
A cup of tea.
You make me hot
When I am cold.
You're all I need
When I grow old.

Serotonin

Defy me now.
Don't you dare!
I control your
Every care.
I'm the one
Who keeps you down.
I'm the one
Who makes you frown.

Mauve is My Favorite Color

We should always do our best
But we don't always do
That which we were sent here for.
I know this much is true.
When you do what's best for them,
You do what's best for you.
Altruism is a selfish thing
But in a subtle hue.

The "Torcher"

It's too late to turn back now.
We only can pretend
That we did what we thought we should.
We knew it had to end.
Even though I may take up
With a Johnny-come-lately,
You know deep inside my heart
I still miss you greatly.

"Divine Comedies"

Depression is a way of life
I don't understand.
It comes and goes with impunity.
I do the best I can
To make the most of every day
I'm free of its symptoms.
But, when I can't, I resolve
To watch some good sitcoms.

A Sign of the Times

I love my kitties.
They don't speak.
But they tell me
What they seek.
I've learned their language.
I'm now fluent.
I know what is
Incongruent.

District 101

I went to a public school.
I didn't learn a thing
Except that *my* Golden Rule
Had a special ring:
Do unto others as they do unto you.
Always take their cue.
And never forget (I humbly submit)
It might benefit you.

Prologue to *My Autobiography*

If you stroke my ego,
Surely you will find,
It's too big for anyone
To easily define.
If measured in gazillions,
It would be a "ten."
It's been so long since I began
I don't know where or when.

In the Corner Stoned

They told me, "I'd be sorry,"
And "I told you so."
But why does anyone
Even have to know
I was once a delinquent
Composing silly rhyme
Standing in the corner
Having a good time?

A Sigh of the Times

I love my kitties,
And they love me.
But we don't engage
In repartee.
It goes without saying
We understand
Each other like Alice-
In-wonderland.

No Pain, No Gain: "The Opium of the Masses"

When the night has gone
And the light of day
Come peeking through the clouds
That melt along the way,
You begin to feel
The glimmerings of pain
Of love and loss and lethargy
And all that does remain.

The Altercation

Alas, my dear, you have gone,
Gone so far away.
But you'll be back tomorrow
For you could never stray
Longer than one day
Or one lonely night
Although it is a fact
It was a bitter fight.

"The Flash"

After all is said and done
And the end is near,
Most of what I said to you
Soon will disappear.
Everything must come to pass.
Everyone must die.
That is why I sing to you
One last lullaby.